SOULFUL

The Journey of a Seeker

Mridula Sankhyayan

BookLeaf Publishing
India | USA | UK

"Poetry is the spontaneous overflow of powerful emotions!" These inspiring words from my father, Shri Chandra Mohan Sharma, set me on a journey that unfolded a poet's heart. I dedicate this work to those who have walked the winding path of self-discovery, and to those who are just beginning their journey. May these poems be a source of comfort, inspiration, and guidance. May you find the courage to listen to your own heart, and follow its whispers into the unknown.

Acknowledgement

To the Divine Spark within me, which ignited the flame of curiosity and guided me on this journey of self-discovery.

To my loved ones: my sons, Rishi and Arryan, and my mom, Mrs. Uma Sharma, who have supported and encouraged me, throughout this creative process.

My spiritual Guru, Sri Shivam ji, and Dr. Arun Shankar Narain, who was my first inspiration after my father, Shri Chandra Mohan Sharma, to write.

To the unknown, the unseen, and the unspoken, may these poems be a humble tribute to the mysteries that lie beyond the reaches of our mortal understanding.

And to you, dear reader, may these poems be a reminder that you are not alone on your own journey of self-discovery, and that the spark within you is always guiding you home.

Preface

In the depths of our being, a spark within us yearns to awaken. A spark that beckons us to embark on a journey of self-discovery, to explore the uncharted territories of our soul. This journey, though unique to each individual, is a universal quest for meaning, purpose, and connection with something greater than ourselves.

Soulful: The Journey of a Seeker is a poetic odyssey that chronicles the twists and turns of my inner journey. Through these poems, I invite you to join me on this path of exploration, as we navigate the realms of love, loss, longing, and liberation.

As you embark on this poetic journey with me, I hope that you will find resonance, solace, and inspiration within these pages and a reminder that you are not alone on your own journey, and that the spark within you is always guiding you home.

Touch of a Master's feather

A gentle touch, a whiff of wind
That blew my mind, but held my soul
To feel the wisdom, to seek the freedom
Instill you in me, me in you
Together we fly, through earth and sky
I feel your love, deep and divine
Let me be the string of your guitar
Play its tune, the music beyond time
I meet myself in silence
I bury the past forever,
Its fatigue, its shadows, its violence
I manifest my purpose, compassion alights
As I sink into myself to find your deep insight

Then time stops still, and
We are one, eternally tethered
Still and centred and lit
By the touch of a Master's feather.

The Voice Within

In deep silence,
it speaks to me,
the voice that sees me—
my every thought and action,
my tears and my joys.
It guides me, and I feel the flow;
all feels well in the morning glow.
But when my mind gets cluttered
with myriad voices and noises,
the voice faints, and I hear it no more.
I start to lose myself, bit by bit—
this disconnection with self
brings sorrows and despair.
Everything seems dark and unfair.
Then I remember the voice within,
always waiting for my attention.
In deep silence,

it speaks to me,
the voice that sees me—
and I am whole again.

Who am I?

I am a belief in my creator's mind,
manifesting each day as I lazily unwind.

I am a fleeting thought in this universe—
today I am here, tomorrow, I disperse.

I am a bundle of sporadic feelings—
happy, sad, and glad; at times anxious and
reeling.

I am words released, like arrows from a bow—
compassionate and inspiring, fierce, fiery, and
alarming.

Who am I, I ask of you - all of these, but none
too.

I am energy manifesting, a beauty under
endless blue.

In a Buddha's heart, I am peace permeating.
In this magical existence, I am love in the
making.

Nature's Child

Standing atop a hill,
Gazing at the green valley, still—
The shimmer of a lake,
The breeze soft on my face.

Fills my heart and soul,
Nature playing its role.
Its imperfect perfection,
Nurturing me in pure inaction.

In our daily doing,
Are we gaining or losing?
In alignment, and letting go,
Feel nature's flow.

Nothing to do,

Nowhere to go,
Yet its abundance unfolds,
From our hollow burrows.

Mighty Soul Speaks

My infinitely chattering mind
has written many fictional storylines—
creative, imaginative, and curious,
yet fidgety, fearful, and often dubious.

Many Pygmalion dreams have manifested—
some happy, some nightmare-infested.
"Dream on," speaks the voice of the soul,
but beware the pull of the whirling black
hole.

Drawn to the darkness, as we are,
don't step on to it's melting tar.
Look to the sunshine, within and afar,

energy rising to the seventh star.

And the chatter dies,
as I lay beneath the night skies.
the silence slowly peaks,
when the mighty soul speaks.

Spiritual Love

Falling in love—
Longing, wanting, needing—
A shoulder to cry on
When your heart is weeping.

Romantic dates,
Indulging traits,
Mesmerising moonlit talks—
The knight in shining armour waits.

Many a love of mortals dissolve,
As we rise in spiritual love to evolve.
No falling, only rising in love,
Whispered a mystical white dove.

Compassion, care, and healing—
Uplifting energies revealing.
I stand by your side,

Take my hand on this joyful ride.

Sound of Silence

A humming heart
in silence speaks,
and tells no tales
but listens deep.

The chirp of birds,
and swaying of trees,
a rising sun,
and a gentle breeze.

There is a seer
beyond the senses five.
In the still waters within,
I take an easy dive.

My forehead throbs
as our hearts expand.

I feel every cell singing
The silent song of a mystic band.

Three Sins

I am your protector
Do as I say.
This world is dark as night;
I am your shining light.
It's the Ego that plays the games.

Looking at someone shine
Makes my heart whine.
Why do they have what I don't?
Why don't I have what they do?
Envy and comparisons pull you low.

What will you build
If you are drowning in guilt?
It's a termite that eats you alive.

Let go of thoughts that fester in grime;
Step out, be light, and nurture purity in time.

Mother

When I feel sad and lonely,
God says, "Let there be love only,"
and He makes her heart beat for me.

When the world seems full of sorrow,
My days are dark and hollow,
He talks through her gentle care.

When life feels like a noisy burrow,
He says, "Let the music flow."
He sings to me through her melody.

When for God my heart cries,
And I feel His painful absence,
He smiles in my mother's presence.

Mother to me, is love, care, and melody,
Sent by God, she is my angelic buddy.

I am whole

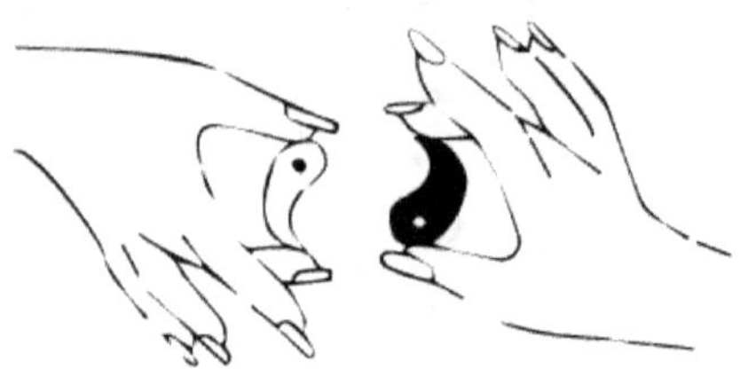

Into the softness of night,
She curls up,
Heart heavy, sleep light.

The buzz of the busy world
Chips away at the silence of my soul.
My whole life crumbles into a soup bowl.

Beneath this chaos,
There is a deep sea of healing,
That speaks to my unsaid feelings.

Your words say I am safe,
I am healed, and I am whole.
You are the master of my soul.

Misfit Mystic

That deep, mesmerising gaze—
A shimmer of love or piercing ablaze,
My soul was held with deep compassion,
A moment of reckoning, life's original
passion.

Love so vast it can't be possessed,
So deep in its silence,
So childlike, playful,
So utterly confusing.

No rules of this game—
Today bane is tomorrow's boon.
It's a roller coaster, freewheeling,
My head is spinning and reeling.

Mind-bending reality,

All myths broken,
Boomerang of an elastic,
That's the touch of a misfit mystic.

The Pathless Path

Finding Self
Am I lost?
What have I lost?
My memory, my awareness, my
knowingness—
All these are words
On life's complex tapestry,
Woven in random forms.
There may be patterns,
But will they repeat?
No one knows.
Repeating patterns don't help
To find the self.
What does?
A walk, a talk, a leap of faith,
Into the unknown,
Onto a pathless land.

No footsteps in the sand,
Just a whisper, a silent awareness,
That I am home.

Dilemma

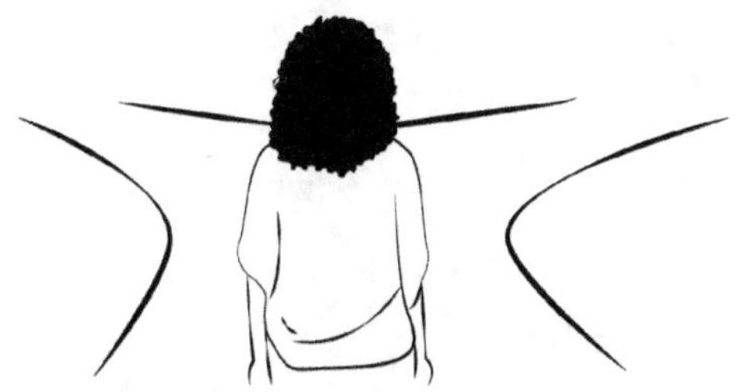

Crossroads of thoughts
Stand there too long,
And be engulfed—
Be drowned in a web so strong.

Right or left, up or down,
Wherever I turn,
Whatever I do,
I see your frown.

Choices are many,
But truth is only One
I bury my past, forget my future—
My present is what I have won.

What is the dilemma,
If I seize this moment now?
I live in bliss,

A path guided by Tao.

Mind Chatter

Listen to the rustling leaves,
Swaying trees.
Listen to the wind blow,
High on the mountain, and the valley below.

A sense of peace prevails,
Expansive and wholesome,
Filling my heart with love,
Feeling full and whole.

Listen to the chatter of the mind—
Voices talking, emotions arising.
In thoughts, we may experience violence;
Pause, and listen to the voice of silence.

Dive deeper into nothingness,
Where love prevails,
And light awaits
Your final lifting of the veils!

Music at the food court

Jingles everywhere,
The dance of silverware.
Warm white plates,
Smoking dishes.

The whoosh of a coffee machine,
The swoosh of a dosa counter,
A smiling chef,
The cleaner's mess.

People chattering,
Children clambering,
The rattling plates
Create sonic waves.

Noise or music?
Music or noise?

If you listen silently,
Music is your choice.

Heart like a River

When life feels stuck and stagnant,
Go sit by a river, be silent.
Watch its unstoppable flow,
Hitting the boulders, daring to go.

Sit by the river side,
Watch it shimmer in twilight.
Feel its soothing touch—
A heavy heart turns light with love.

Open your heart to the Milky Way,
The stars are calling upon you.
Feel the love, as you rejoice and sway,
Let the love flow, as the river meets the bay.

Step into the unknown, leave your cover.
Fear not, even if you quiver.

Allow the love to flow through you,
Blessed are you with a heart like a river.

Presence

An enigmatic wave
Swept my being,
Held my heart,
Caressing me within.

A tingling feeling,
Like jingle bells
Ringing in my ears—
Twinkling eyes, she tells.

Darkness melts away,
Negative imprints fade faster.
The light inside, like morning sunshine,
That's the presence of a Master Divine.

Love

Her eyes had a faraway gaze,
Her fingers played with the lace.
A gentle smile,
A warm heart on the line—
Love is waiting for the beloved entwined.

Lovingly cooking a meal,
Changing linens, fresh and clean.
An extra blanket or a cushion,
Taking care is his daily mission.
Love is an act of kindness in motion.

Possessing is not love;
What makes them happy is.
No terms, just letting them fly free.
In this moment, I wholeheartedly love thee.

Love is being there and letting go.

Slippery Slopes

I see them come alive
In the memory bank where I dive,
My dreams and my fondest hopes,
Around the corners of slippery slopes.

A brother once was,
Bearing that cross,
Makes my heart pause,
Love, laughter, and heavy loss.

Relationships - she mopes,
How they twist, O how they turn!
Tightening nooses, entangled ropes,
Beware, life is a bend of slippery slopes.

The Rising

I can feel the rising within,
In the chants of a monk,
In the temple bell's clunk,
In the dancing sun rays' spunk.

In the silence of meditation,
On a sleepy summer railway station,
I can feel the rising
As the jungle birds sing.

In the presence of a Master,
The rising moves faster.
Surrender to the magic within,
Stay aware and tuned in.

When the rising reaches the heart,
The eyes well up, energy darts.
I embrace your presence,
Crowning glory, life's essence.

Shunya

A state of non-doing,
Standstill, and blissful being,
Gently sliding within,
Infusing the energies
For chakra healing.
The first state of non-doing,
Grounded, stable, and knowing.
The delight of creativity and sensing,
The sacral chakra's doing.
In a silent mind, the self-doubt dies;
The solar plexus acts, and my confidence
ignites.
Experiencing the flow of energy,
Into my heart, flowing like a river of love,
My expression comes alive;

I speak and teach, finding fulfillment above.
The third eye vibrates;
I dive deeper, intuition resonates.
Peaking at the crown,
I am spirit, I am love,
I am energy,
I am all and none!

Living to Dead

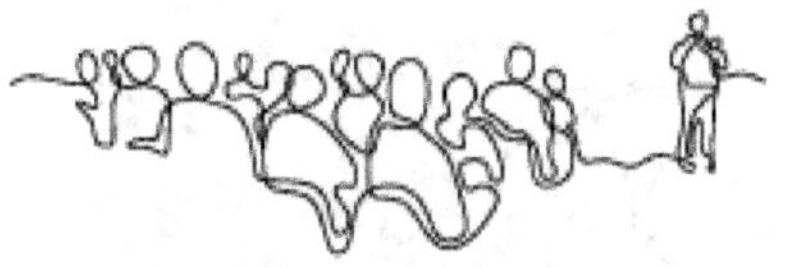

We are all strung to the same thread of life,
Wandering lost within the maze,
Happy, blissful, and ignorant,
Until the pangs of hunger strike.
Pangs of hunger, of different kinds,
For some, it is food; for some, it is fun.
Some crave love while others seek lust,
Power for many, even pain for some.
And then for a few it is a quest, a search,
diving, deep within, a soul connect.
Into the light, now they see the thread,
As they walk the path from living to dead.

Aura of Love

I like to peep from the valley below,
The setting golden disk of the sun,
The silver lining of the clouds,
The rainbow colors, sweet and soft.
Down in the valley, in the silent valley,
I saw the maddening joys of spring,
Sprightful dancing on the glossy slopes,
With my sweet dreams and fondest hopes.
My senses swimming in ecstasy,
Full of poetry and colors,
Flowers and fragrance,
My thoughts wandering with the
Murmuring sound of a buzzing bee,
Bursting forth.. seeking no bound.
In the awe of nature and its creation,
Thoughts pass away into a sweet nothingness,
Leaving behind the exotic perfume-

The fragile fragrance of tender emotions,
The heightening awareness of deep set love.

Lost in Love or Loved and Lost

My beauty lies in your eyes, love,
Sometimes you see it, sometimes you don't.
Today I feel beautiful and warm,
As if my friends are watching over me.
Sometimes you care to see deep within,
Yet often you love me on the surface.
Today, I hope, it's not my clothes
That took your breath away.
Just a little deeper, the joys of spring,
A ring of April's song,
Moments I have lost but still for them I long.
Love forever and pain went in vain

Anguish, fear, and frustration,
All of them emotions
They dwell within like a melting pot.
Will you carry my burden? But how could
you?
You are already bent deep under yours.
Is that why, in the company of our dearest
friends,
We often feel so alone?

Charisma Never Ends

The charisma never ends,
The feelings flow to touch the charm,
And the only verse rings in my heart:
Break forth into joy, O my soul.
It's a strange mixture—
The pleasure of ample joy,
The pain of a broken heart.
I am bound to my own ties and
And to your vibrations.
When the auras match,
The feelings seek no bounds.
Sometimes the expression comes alive,
And sometimes it shies away

For reasons unknown.
He thinks it's love,
She calls it infatuation.
I think it's that precious something—
That once-in-a-lifetime
Breathes into you the warmth
And stays forever.

CANVAS

When the sky is blue
And the sun is shining through,
When all you hear is the sound of music
That carries the river's flow.

Overlooking the river, he stands by her side,
With his feet sunk into the soft velvet grass.

She awaits him patiently... eagerly.

A gust of breeze
Sends a shiver down her naked body.
She quivers as he sets his eyes on her,
The warmth of his honeydew eyes
Sweeps over her golden-white figure.

He reaches to touch her gently,
His fingers vibrant to her satin feel.

"It's me you are waiting for,"
She knows her moment has come.
As he picks up the brush,

It's her moment of delight,
As she gets fulfilled
By her painters' choicest colors.

Soul Searching

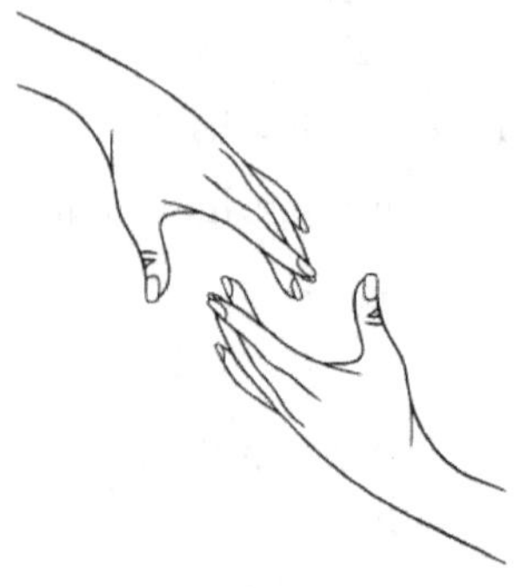

I had travelled much in time, through seasons
galore,
Lived a million lives, died a million deaths.
Each moment was precious, I gave it my all.
I lived it to the fullest, and died in it, never to
be born again.
I felt like I had never felt before.

It was the song of my life, and its music was
my soul.
It was my inner strength.

Winters came and went; I stood like a rock.
I felt no chill in my bones.

In dust and heat, I turned to a desert
That would burn tender feet.

In thunder and storm, I grew into a forest
To guard the land and farm.

It was the song of my life, and its music was
in my soul.
It was my will to be and become all.
I felt like I had never felt before.

With thoughts of yesteryears, I have travelled
back in time,
To the ancient city of my soul,
The sand of the desert has swept away;
The forest is now but a few barren trees,
The rock bears cracks like an aged face.

It was the song of my life; it has music no
more.
I feel like I have never felt before.
Down on my knees, shaken, tired, and
begone...

Come to me, O master of heavens.
Look at me with a little love; I will smile with
the twinkle of stars above.
Hold me, and I will melt away in your arms.
Kiss me, and you will breathe in me the song
of my soul.
I will feel like I have never felt before.

Moments with the Rock

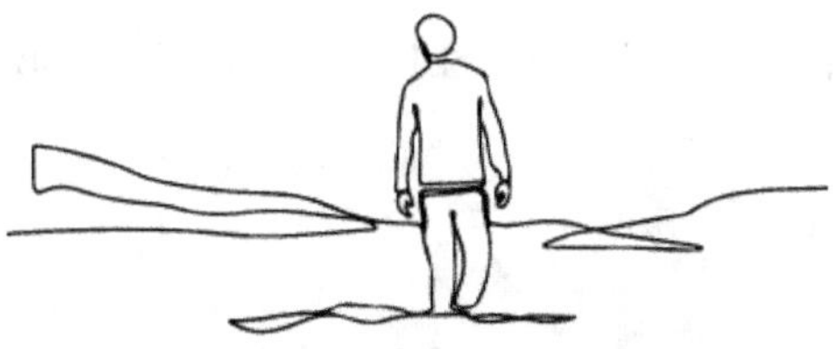

Those precious moments...
Moments that were precious even then!
They seem dearer than diamonds and pearls
today.
They twinkle bright, or light at times,
But always linger at the top of my mind.
Whatever I do, wherever I go,
Feelings just follow through.
Sometimes they ignite with pulse and passion,
And often they sink in the depths of emotion.

I stand like a rock, because I chose to.
I smile through the days sunshine,
And crumble into a dark foliage of the jungle
night.
The tears spring out in wilderness,
Shining brightly like the dew drops on
forlorn woods.

No one notices as the day grows.
The heat of the hour dries the dew drops,
Yet the rock stands still, facing the scorching sun,
Because I chose to.

Caged Canary

When you sing a sad song, O Lark!
It flows through my whole being.
I feel it sink in me, deep and dark,
In a lost corner of my heart.

I hear the flutter of a canary,
Hitting hard against the caged prison.
Till the wings grow strong, and the will to
last,
It hits and hits to soar to its freedom.

So I open the caged doors.
Fly away, fly away, my Canary.
I have set you free,
But the canary stays still.

Why won't you fly, my Canary?
Your sad eyes hold me for a long moment,
Say nothing. I know your plight.
Canary, I see my reflection in your eyes.

Days Gone By...

I often go back to those magic moments
When life was bountiful and charming.
When on my tender feet, I chased
'Blacky,' the goat in my grandma's garden.
When I laughed loud and often,
And though I spilt a few teardrops,
They never ever stained my heart.
Mornings shone sunshine on my shoulders,
And evenings were a song.
Life was simple, and I loved it all.

Now I am older and wiser.
The garden is a lone patch of green;
Grandma and Blacky have gone away.

I tread carefully through the nooks and
corners
And think before I smile.
Mornings slip fleetingly by, and
Evenings are a sad reminder of days gone by...

The future is yet a distant dream.
Perhaps I will sow a few seeds this spring,
In my grandma's patch of green.
Standing barefoot in the garden of fond
memories,
I feel my tender feet again.

Ashes to Ashes, Dust to Dust

So many skeletons buried,
And yet you want to drown again—
Drown in those unusually lovely eyes,
Drown not to swim but to die,
Only to be buried again.
Dust your soul of its sinful ways,
Or dust be yourself, be thy grave.

The sacrificial goat says to the masters of the
sword:
"Would he ever feel the same,
Or my blood will flow in vain?"

In vain it is, you naïve woman,
You've fallen forever
Under the curse of 'Satan.'

I am begging for forgiveness.
Mysterious are the ways of love;
Falling for an angel was no choice of mine.
But I will hold the fire in the dark of my
heart—
I will burn in its passion like a funeral pyre.

For when his heart weeps for a lover's must,
It'll serve my existence, ashes to ashes, dust to
dust!

Shades of Life

A bit of sun for every soul,
A patch of sky that I call mine,
A little breeze caught in my hair,
A few raindrops that wet my face.

As I hang over my balcony,
Letting my thoughts flow,
I held on to the most of
Every bit of life I got.

When life doesn't flow spontaneously,
When it doesn't come in leaps and bounds,
Then every moment is treasured,
And every bit is dear.

I cherish every such shade of the day,

Forever to make it stay—
Every shade that is rich and thoughtful with a
divine hue,
Every shade that is share with you.

Time is passing by

When you are running too fast
And buzzing like a busy bee,
When there is too much to do and
Not a moment free,
It's a whirlwind around you.
You try to stand tall as a tree,
But you are not tall enough,
And whirlwind's too strong.
You are swept off your feet,
Spinning round and round,
But it's not a merry-go-round—
For I hear no kids' laughter.
My fast asleep
As I tiptoe from my work.

It's an early morning flight tomorrow,
From today, a few moments can I borrow?
Misty-eyed, sitting on my flight,
I missed kissing my lil one good night.
"Sleep tight, don't let the bedbugs bite."
There was no good morning, darling, either.
I did not see his smile today, he did neither.
A hug, a smile, a kiss, I am gonna miss.
Capture the moment, hold that thought,
Hug him to bliss.
For time is ticking, and moments are passing
by.
Go live your life with your life
Before you say goodbye.

God's Magic

God's magic is around us,
In beautiful ways, it surrounds us.
When the waterfall turns white,
Our worries become feather-light.
When flowers bloom,
I enjoy a sleepy summer afternoon.
When skies are adorned with silver moon,
God is humming a beautiful tune.
When it's drizzling rain,
God is wiping away our pain.
When the rainbow follows the sunny, cloudy skies,
God's painted for our hearts and eyes.
When deserts grow melons,
And mountains stand tall with pine groves,
I thank God for His love,
In wonderful ways He shows.
God's magic is around us
If we are ready to receive,
It will find us...

Into the Hollow of my Heart

Into the hollow of my heart,
You fill it the rainbow colors.
Today, as you dwell in my thoughts,
And blossom every day in the flower pots.
Marigold has never shone brighter before,
Glistening leaves on roadside trees
Never seemed so divine and pure.
Is it you pouring your love around?
In a distant land, we shall be found,
For sure, once again, to share
Love, laughter, joy, and care.

Love you, always and forever...

As Soul Journeys
Through

Silencing the cacophony of myriad emotions,
Going beyond the superficiality of relations,
When the light shines on deep waters,
Beyond the ripples and their silver
reflections,
Do you not sense the essence of life?
As the soul journeys through...

As I Walk into your Divinity

As I walk into your divinity,
The quintessential journey of you and me,
Travelling through time, matter ,and energy,
Manifesting flora, fauna, birds, and bees.

They walk into our love and light,
Living the warm glow and smiling bright,
Transcending beliefs, ritual, and rites.

And the beauty manifests in moonlit night,
The incoming waves of passion ignite,
In the awakening of the Goddess, they both
unite.

The timeless journey of you and me,
Through Earth and the Milky Galaxy,
Varying forms of matter, the same energy.

I see you, you see me,
Into the oneness of you and me!
Through infinity, until eternity!

I walk into your divinity!

Internet of Beings

It's a one-way ticket
To the station: Internet.
You say it, but you don't hear it back.
Everyone is so busy talking,
No one is listening.

Chit chat, chatter, and no friendly banter.
Beep beep beep, chit-chat, chatter.
No one is talking,
Yet messages are raining, but no one is
soaking.

No one listens to my heart's ache.
Like or smiley is easy to fake.
Social media prisoners, even those who care,
Share, share, like, like, post, post.
Wiki is my bestie and my host.

Who did I notice, who noticed me?
It's time to change my selfie.
How am I trending, honey bee?
And who is trending faster than me?

No one is listening to the sound of my voice,
To the beat of my heart, to my dream;
To my silence, to my aches and pains,
To my bumpy ride, to my lonely night.

No one listens, and no one can understand.
A thousand friends, but no one to hold my
hand.
I am human, floating in the cloud,
A virtual cloud of love, hugs, likes, and
frowns,
Craving for a human touch.
Am I asking for too much?

As the violet turns blue

The violet skies, deep and dark,
A gush of cool breeze
Played with my scarf.

The day is yet to dawn.
I await thee, my angel,
Barefoot in the lawn.

The music has begun
As I flutter my wings,
Race to the skies as one.

One with you, so true,
We dance with the moves
As the violet turns blue.

Whisper of wind and cool of dew,
Honey-sweet breath,
She says, "I love you."

Eternal Query

Staying alive to the eternal query...
What's my purpose, who am I and what I
ought to be...
Where have I come from and where am I
headed...
Who has the answers, who could tell me..
Lost in the woods, I am no Alice.
I am lost in the clutter of my jumbled
thoughts;
They have grown a jungle and lost the paths.
Lost, lost, lost, only to be found
With a deeper meaning of eternal life!
Found on a path.. that's homeward bound!

To Love is to Be

Who else can you have this conversation with
If not with God Himself?
His love knows no bounds!
I seek and I seek, and He gives and He gives—
Unbound, ever-flowing, filling up my heart
And letting it overflow, still pouring over.
He flows, I flow, he loves, I love, it's beyond compare.
This dance of the divine is so joyous and mesmerising
That I melt into sweet nothingness.
I lose myself to love and just love remains.
Then I give and I give and I give and I give,
Just love, His love that flows through me.
I know nothing else but to give in His love,
In the name of His love. To love is to be!

Set my Spirit free

Rooted to the ground,
I want to spread my wings and fly,
Listen to the hush of the wind,
The rustle of the leaves, reaching the sky.
Soft grass beneath my feet,
The scent of a spring flower so sweet—
My incredible bodhi tree,
Set my spirit free...